**To all those people
whose tomorrows
will not be like
their yesterdays were.**

Other Books by Tom Payne

From the Inside Out:
How to Create and Survive a Culture of Change

A Company of One:
The Power of Independence in the Workplace

FutureWork:
Five Rules for a New Game

Quotes
for a changing workplace

TOM PAYNE

𝗣𝗣
Performance Press of Albuquerque

Quotes

for a Changing Workplace

Copyright © 1998 Thomas E. Payne

All rights reserved. Written permission to reproduce parts of this book may be requested from LODESTAR. See page 136.

Publisher's Cataloging in Publication Data

Payne, Thomas E.
Quotes for a Changing Workplace

1. Success in business. 2. Employee motivation. 3. Organizational Change.

HD 58.9.P66   1998   658.4   97-69849
ISBN 0-9627085-7-7 $9.95   Soft Cover

Cover Design: Dave Payne - Hodge Podge Lodge
Cover Photo: Kim Jew Photography Studios

Printed in the United States of America

Quantity discounts available - see page 136.

Dear Reader,

Changes are everywhere. In a few short years our organizations have moved from massive downsizing to record high employment. On the job we have experienced security, loyalty and individual effort being replaced by independence, mobility and teams. In working since 1983 with the multitudes going through changes, big and small, voluntary and non-voluntary, much got said that is worth saving and savoring.

These quotes were chosen from my books, speeches and workshops to generate dialogue, stimulate debate and explore an excitingly different relationship with our work.

Change doesn't care what we think of it, but we had better care what we think. The following pages are full of thinking stuff.

Tom Payne

Quotes...
___

If what we are doing at work does not fill
our beings with passion, it had better
fill our wallets with money.

Dependency on organizations we may be forced to change several times generates negative stress.

The choice of how our life is balanced will be made. If we don't make the choice, then something else will.

Quotes...

If we believe our lack of success occurred as a result of the action of someone or something outside of us, then someone or something outside of us will have to change for us ever to succeed.

Deposit often in the trust bank; you never can tell when you'll need a withdrawal.

I'm not a trained therapist, but I do give myself some credit for common sense, and using the past to determine what we can or can not be in the future is not common sense.

There is nothing as stimulating in an organization as everybody communicating honestly with each other.

Quotes...

Considering the volatility and opportunity in the job market, there should not be one employable person without an updated résumé or its equivalent.

If we choose what words mean to us, can't we choose not to be hurt by them?

Advancing technology may do more to enhance certain relationships, by nullifying inconsequential physical differences we've been fighting and agonizing over during our lifetime, than any of the social programs of the last 100 years.

Things don't happen to teach us something. Things just happen, and any learning is ours to ferret out.

Quotes...

I believe we are treated by others the way we have taught others to treat us. I also believe that we are treated by our organizations the way we have taught our organizations to treat us. How are you teaching your organization to treat you?

Both the employee and the organization must be ready to do without each other at a moments notice.

When moving toward self-reliance, the destination of our trip does not cause fear as much as the trip itself.

Consider the futility of a life when we're not happy with the game we're playing, yet choose to continue playing.

Quotes...

To be successful we must recognize candidly our level of responsibility for the events that occur in our lives and accept total responsibility for how we react to those events.

People who are like each other tend to like each other, but you don't have to like people to work with them.

When do we, as humans, generally hit our "laugh peak?" I've never read any such study, but if there were a study on that, would you bet the answer would be - ten years old or 40 years old? Why?

What we have learned, we can unlearn. Unfortunately when it comes to our fears, we tend to learn quickly and unlearn slowly.

Quotes...

Everyone in the final analysis is in business for him or her self, always was and always will be.

Did you ever notice how many people are worried about losing jobs they didn't want in the first place and don't much like now?

What we give with our work is every bit as important as what we get from it.

We don't think about more things than we think about. So we leave alot of what could potentially make a much better us unthought about. Think about that.

Quotes...

When the employees are committed to a vision they believe has meaning, if the leader leaves, the employees still have a sense of direction and passion and can operate independently.

When you're developing your mission statement, if you can't stay in business without a positive bottom line, for gosh sake, say it!

Did the founders of your organization have an idea, garner capital, adhere to all the government regulations, hire a bunch of strangers, negotiate for real estate, and experience many sleepless nights all for the purpose of making you happy?

Quotes...

The easiest way for people to embrace change is if they see the benefit as personal, immediate and certain. The least enticing is when they feel the benefit of change is primarily organizational, delayed and a gamble.

Assume that 80 percent of the negative attitude toward change rests with 20 percent of the change.

The organizations of today are faced with the independence paradox. They need independent people who are dependent.

If your main goal is security, you will always act with caution, and in a dynamic organization that can only survive by taking risks, your being fired could become a self-fulfilling prophecy.

Quotes...

When we look outside of ourselves for someone or something to help us become independent, we're looking in the wrong direction.

Fear doesn't come as part of the human package. We add it as an option. Be selective.

We would believe everything if we could, but we can't.

★

All of us together know things none of us know apart.

★

If we don't control our organizations, is it in our best interest to be dependent upon them?

Quotes...

Organizations may fear educating a mobile work force, and employees may perceive it a waste of time to educate themselves for jobs that might disappear. Such thinking is both short-sighted and critically flawed.

If you're not sure of the importance of the simple act of listening, think back to the last time you were really listened to. It's an almost religious experience.

Keep in mind that, for its financial good, the organization could and would dump you in a blink of an eye.

It's said that only when we can visualize something can we make it happen. If this is true, then so must the opposite be true. If we can't visualize something, we can't make it happen.

Quotes...

Personal growth and increased confidence take place when we are testing the limits of our lives.

Ponder this sobering thought concerning today's organizational reality — Your organization doesn't care what your plans are!!

There is an obvious reason why so many people do not think of the relevance of mission to personal and organizational success. That reason is: 99.857 percent of the employees couldn't say what the organization's mission was if their lives depended on it.

We, as workers, accepted the condition of dependency on our organizations, and we must now eliminate it.

Quotes...

Once the structure as we know it is gone, organizations are flattened, and workers are self-reliant, mission may be the only realistic way to insure everyone is pointed in the same direction.

Any time we allow ourselves to put forth less than our best effort, we know it, and that to some degree diminishes us in our own minds.

For the good of us all and the strength of our relationships, we must encourage others to confront us, to push against us and to test our conviction at every turn. That's a healthy relationship.

If we're not self-confident enough to take care of ourselves, who do we think is going to take care of us?

Quotes...

If we don't tighten up our processes and maximize our technology, our competition will eat our lunch, and we could lose our jobs. If we do tighten up our processes and maximize our technology, our organizations will not need as many people, and we could — lose our jobs!

Maybe we should exercise just because we can.

What are the basics of management, teamwork, communications, sales and customer service, all essential for organizational productivity, if not the relationships of human beings?

It has been determined that hunting and gathering societies only spent 15 to 20 hours per week "working." You can bet the subject of "balance of life" was not often bandied about the campfire.

Quotes...

Rejecting responsibility comes easily because, if we do accept responsibility, then we have to admit the person we are today is one chosen by us.

The goal of interdependence between employee and organization is realistic. To think it will happen in our work life is unrealistic considering all the baggage most of us carry around on our jobs.

Moments, the instant they're lived, become our past. The instant before they're lived, they're our future. Our power is in the present.

If you were a tightrope walker, would you be more interested in performing every move to the best of your ability if you had a safety net? Would you try harder if you didn't have one?

Quotes...

What's done is done and can't be undone. What's to be done is to be done, and it's up to us to do it.

To survive and flourish in the world of tomorrow, the question is not if an organization adopts a culture of employee self-responsibility, the question is when.

In the world of the three-armed, the two-armed is handicapped.

Maybe the only real responsibility of an organization is to provide a safe place to work and an honest day's wage for an honest day's work. The reality is the employees provide the rest.

Quotes...

Fear is a learned emotion. We learn to fear everything we fear except fears of falling, loud noises and a legislature in session.

As soon as each worker realizes the only security that does exist is within him or herself and prepares for and can visualize a future without the company, then the worker can truly choose to be a participating member of the organization.

If we can not get excited for, passionate about
and committed to what we do for a living,
we lose nothing of real importance
when we don't do it anymore.

Quotes...

We can't let others judge our quality of life, nor, as tempting as it may be, should we judge the quality of others' lives.

Organizations should be creating motivational environments necessary to keep those employees who choose to work rather than creating fear techniques for those employees who perceive they have to work.

If management can get somebody to quickly react to fear motivation, they'd be foolish not to use it. Don't play that game.

Develop a short memory for your failures and a long memory for successes.

Quotes...

Holding ourselves responsible for what we make of our lives is simple — we're 100 percent responsible.

The events in our lives don't determine the quality of our lives; our reactions to those events do.

Was it more painful to be dragged kicking and screaming into the factories of yesterday or dragged kicking and screaming out of the factories of today?

Independent people benefit from their independence because they possess the ability to act on their own hopes and dreams, not somebody else's.

Quotes...

Waiting for someone or something else to change for us to become as successful as we wish to be can be frustrating at best and paralyzing at worst.

How many of us are "doing more with less," "doing better faster," and "sticking 12 hours of work in a ten-hour bag," to insure we have "things," and then don't appreciate what we have?

If you want to work, you can right now. If you're looking for a job, it might take awhile.

To get something we don't have, we must give up something we do have.

Quotes...

If we don't believe we possess or can get the skills necessary to succeed in the future, and we choose to work there, we're putting ourselves in a tough position.

To find out how to get where you're going, you have to know where you are. To get to the future, we must know the present.

If I had to choose either skills or attitude — I'd take skills.

★

Listen to others for ideas not doctrine. What works for you, works for you.

★

To not know your possibilities is the same as not having any.

Quotes...

To <u>not</u> want something to happen is as good a motivator as to want something to happen. Fear motivates as effectively as desire.

Take care of yourself. You have more interest in that project than anybody else.

Self-confident people may have this irresistible urge to work harder. Remember, working for an organization is now their idea. They're working because they want to.

Many children look at their parents and see lives that revolve around four events: the weekend, vacation, retirement and death. What do your children see?

Quotes...

Downsizing corrects the mistakes of the past, but it's not designed to create the future. Something else has to do that.

Like it or not, reality is being fired at us point blank. All jobs are temporary — always were and always will be — but there will always be work.

There was a time we did not exist.
Now we do exist.
There will come a time we do not exist again.
How are we making the second time we didn't exist better than the first time we didn't exist?

Quotes...

You have to be self-confident on the inside before you can be self-confident on the outside.

Our purpose is no longer simple. Do we sell sea shells by the seashore, or sell floor space in Cyberspace?

If we relinquish responsibility, we give up control of our lives because we are declaring someone or something else is in charge. How scary is that? And we're not only letting it happen; we're making it happen!

To cap employees' emotions is to dam up the passion and energy they have to give to the job.

Quotes...

If we don't like what our organization has become, if we don't like its beliefs, values, culture and respect for people, and if its new mission does not complement our personal purpose; then for the good of the organization and ourselves, we should part company.

Do you have company benefits or do company benefits have you?

What are you willing to do differently to get a different result?

Organizations benefit from an independent workforce because independent people are more able to focus on satisfying the needs of others rather than on worrying about satisfying themselves.

Quotes...

A self-confident person may desire certain affiliations with organizations or relationships with others but does not need them to validate personal existence.

People may do things that benefit others but will commit to things that benefit them.

Organizations can do anything they want with a dependent work force, and dictating change is quicker than selling change.

Security does not lie in the organization but in the quality of one's work.

Quotes...

The more we depend on an external organization to make us secure, happy, fulfilled, productive, and satisfied, the less need or desire we will have to care for ourselves.

Any of us, at any time, for any number of reasons could find ourselves "dehired." But if we know what we really love to do, the turmoil is merely — annoying.

Is our work full of excitement or excrement?

Jobs today are not lost; they're merely misplaced. The economy is playing an interesting, challenging and exciting game of "hide the job."

Quotes...

We will never be really secure as long as we are in business to help other people accomplish their goals. The only true security is when we are in business to accomplish our own goals.

Organizations rent employee skills for as long as the organization needs those skills. Period.

Organizations benefit from an independent workforce because independent people who are not committed to the organization's mission feel able to leave and don't remain to drain limited resources.

If I can do something for others, and they can't do something for me, does that mean I should dump them? Yes.

Quotes...

Boss, get off the executive floor and out of the executive washroom, exit the executive dining room, dash from the executive parking lot, and sit with the people who really know yo5p business. Get involved.

If we know we're going to laugh at our failures sometime, why wait? Laugh when they happen.

Consider all the people who helped mold you into what you are today. Some worked with a polishing rag and others with a sledgehammer, but without those past relationships, today you would be someone else.

Even if one slept soundly during Psychology 101, the pitfalls of asking employees to engage in short-term personal pain for organizational long-term gain are obvious.

Quotes...

Two prerequisites for organizational cultural change, neither of which is considered to be in abundance in many of today's organizations, are time and money.

I'll let you in on a secret — risk taking is easy. It's easy because we don't really take risks. If we thought it was a risk, we wouldn't do it.

Relationship is recognizing the part other people play in our lives and valuing the strength we derive from this connection with the whole.

Trying to be sure everybody likes you is an interesting pastime, considering there are now close to six billion people playing in that game with you. What are your chances?

Quotes...

The past got us to where we're at, but it doesn't have to take us to where we're going.

If work is an activity viewed as a "have to" rather than a "want to," unnecessary limitations are placed on our excitement, passion and commitment.

If we are not independent, we are not as valuable to the team.

It's time we stopped blaming the organization for its suppressive systems and controlling environment and acknowledge the fact that the systems and environment are the cumulative creation of each and every individual who together makes up the organization. If we don't like it — we should change it.

Quotes...

Words by themselves mean nothing.
When we are offended by a word,
might it say more about us
than it does about the word itself?

If the organization is to make significant change, so must the individuals who make it up.

Do we form a relationship based on what others can do for us or for what we can do for others? I say neither. Relationships are based on what we can do for each other.

Quotes...

We get rewarded by society for performing skills effectively and efficiently. Precious few others in our lives seem to care what our dreams are.

The thought of losing rekindles the joy of having.

Will the change you are generating create real growth, or is change being implemented simply because you're not sure what else to do?

What good would it do if we had 100 people in our organization and they were motivated in 50 different directions?

Quotes...

The concept of failure does not disturb people. It's the perceived consequence of failure that disturbs people.

The only true source of security is the self-respect we will feel doing work that to us is meaningful and acting on our own hopes and dreams, not somebody else's.

If the suits in the suites haven't figured out what the organization of the future should look like, why don't the workers take a shot at it?

When organizations say they have trouble communicating, it typically means people aren't telling each other the truth.

Quotes...

Self-esteem is not about winning or losing in the eyes of others. Self-esteem is about taking ourselves to our own personal limits in the areas of our lives we have deemed important.

If we are dependent on an organization but that organization is not dependent on us, the relationship is too one-sided to be healthy.

The reason so many folks tend to blame events outside of themselves for their lot in life is that if it's not someone or something else that's responsible, then there is only one other choice.

Many want the illusion but not the reality of a self-confident workforce.

Quotes...

A major benefit of meditation is we feel just as relaxed and energized as after exercise, and we don't have to take a shower.

Organizations have no emotion; they only have a pocketbook. The heart, soul and passion come from the people who make up the organization.

We are too important and have too much to offer, and life is too short not to do what we love.

Regardless of what Mrs. Conway said in third grade, failure has benefits.

Quotes...

Creating independent employees may well need to be the main focus of employers in the years to come, if business as we know it is to survive.

How we do things tends to change at a greater clip than why we do things. Form often changes; substance rarely does.

The days of the organization providing all the training needs of an employee are gone the way of guaranteed employment. If we need it, we go get it.

Once committed, people need to be committed to what they're committed to.

Quotes...

Before we can win, it's essential we know what game we're playing — not the game we'd like to play, not the game we think we should be playing, but the game we <u>are</u> playing.

How do others benefit from what you do for a living?

The more people focus on what's wrong with what they have, the less they focus on how to fix the situation.

Organizations do what they have to do, and workers do what they have to do.

Quotes...

If it's not the company's objective to keep us employed, whose objective is it?

If we have five pounds of work in a ten-pound spirit, the rattling around will drive us nuts.

Consider the names we give to the beginning and the end of the traditional work week, "Blue Monday" and "Thank God it's Friday." Does that say something?

Intellectually grasping the idea of independence in the workplace is no problem, but we may spend the rest of our lives "getting it" emotionally.

Quotes...

A rich, exciting and vibrant life is the balance between productive and destructive fears — our choice.

You have the answer; listen quietly for the question.

Organizational loyalty is still alive; it's the old definition that's dead.

We are turning into an economy of people with saleable skills and people without.

Quotes...

Organizations (Fortune 500 or sole proprietorships) survive by renting workers' behaviors, time, and physical presence, but organizations thrive when they receive workers' excitement, passion and commitment.

Talk to people who know what they're talking about.

We are not talking about employees becoming independent so they <u>will</u> leave their jobs. We are talking about employees becoming independent so they <u>can</u> leave — critical difference.

Employees will gauge the manager's priorities based upon where the manager spends his or her most valuable commodity — time.

Quotes...

Change will not occur unless it's easier to change than not to change. So why should change bother us?

★

Know the game, master the skills and play to win.

★

You will do the job as you view the job.

If we accept the concept of self-responsibility, the reality is our self-esteem is being set up to be stroked or stomped.

If we get what we think about most, why would we think about what we don't want?

Quotes...

The past and the future are great places to visit, but you don't want to live there.

Work is a means to an end. We must be free to pursue other means at our discretion if our end is not being met.

A self-confident person chooses to do everything he or she does.

If we are not willing to increase the supply of something, for example, employee headcount, then we must increase its yield. With the mood of many workers today, organizations have a big job ahead of them.

Quotes...

If a business does not accomplish its bottom line,
there will be no customers.
Without customers,
employees are a real extravagance.

Workers should not perform behaviors if they do not believe in them.

The reason many people don't like to spend time alone is they don't like the company.

Quotes...

We willingly gave control to our organizations because we believed we were buying security in return. Since we do not have the security we desired, shouldn't we get the control back?

If we don't take responsibility for our results being the way they are, then we won't be inclined to take responsibility for changing those results.

When a person chooses to improve performance, performance will be improved.

Without the highly structured "jobs" of the past and with technology changing our present game by the nanosecond, the future is oozing with endless potential.

Quotes...

Work is not always work, play is not always play, and the lucky ones can't tell the difference.

Is there any rational reason people should be nicer to others than they are to themselves?

Your emotional ties to an organization mean nothing when competing against your organization's business interests.

A true bottom-line orientation has the management aligning with the shareholders. The employees and the customers become costs to contain.

Quotes...

If we identify with an organization and not with our own unique skills, leaving that organization for their reasons or ours will be extremely difficult.

If I could wish one ability for the person focused on succeeding in an ever-changing game, one ability that would provide the most leverage toward success, I would choose — independence

Managers need their people more than their people need the managers.

To have knowledge was a priority for yesterday. To obtain knowledge is a priority for tomorrow.

Quotes...

Are we working for our organizations because we want to or because we have to?

If we're not contributing more than we're costing our organization — we're gone.

Might we have a self-image thermostat we set at a level that is most comfortable for us? We go over and we shut down; under, we crank it up.

Only when we feel free to leave can we freely choose to stay.

Quotes...

How many relationships we let die because we're too busy is our choice, but we must be real sure that what we're busy doing is worth the loss of that relationship.

The prospect of losing job security does not negatively affect those with marketable skills and an independent attitude.

Think about how much fun we forfeit in the present by focusing on what might happen in the future or what did happen in the past. And as a by-product of a past/future focus, we destroy the present.

The results of our lives are with us because there is more benefit to us for having our results as they are, than there is benefit to changing them.

Quotes...

Concentrate on what you're for and forget what you're against; it's wasted energy.

If you can't find your personal purpose on your current job, for the good of all concerned, get out.

When I started talking to different organizations, one of the first things I noticed was most people were not having fun.

If the interest of an individual employee runs up against the interest of the bottom line, the employee loses. We can be disappointed if we want, but being angry doesn't help.

Quotes...

An independent worker is no longer loyal, in the old sense, to a legal entity because the legal entity is not loyal, in the old sense, to him or her.

You can't consciously <u>not</u> focus on something. Try not thinking of that.

What unites us is what we want; what divides us is how to get it.

Looking outside in the light is easy, but it's a good bet the answer is inside, in the dark.

Quotes...

While change provides growth, challenge and learning, it can also be debilitating when served in large chunks.

When analyzing the work we want to do, remember all work is important if it is consistent with our purpose, beneficial to the community and supportive of the environment.

In today's economy, the highly skilled will thrive, the skilled will survive, and the unskilled will dive.

Don't be discouraged about how far you have to go; just look at how far you have come.

Quotes...

Technology drove us to the factories; technology is now driving us away.

People in today's multi-functional, "job-in-a-box" organizations crave the fulfillment of purpose. People in tomorrow's organizations will demand it.

True confidence must follow not precede actual performance.

While even a blind pig roots up an acorn every once in awhile, it's a poor bet that we'll win a game we don't know we're playing.

Quotes...

We can't fear the past.
Fear is a future thing.
And since the future's all in our heads,
fear must be a head thing.

If we are being paid more by our organization than the open market is willing to pay for our skills, we are in deep yogurt.

What's the good of teaching children anything if they're not taught a sense of their own self-worth?

Quotes...

When the organization is done doing what it's doing, are you OK with it? If not, do you see you have a choice?

Just when the company needs creative, innovative, risk-taking, independent people, it's getting a whole immobile employee body more worried about having a job than about doing the job they have.

Self-confident people benefit because they deserve and get both personal and organizational respect.

If we're not willing to take a risk, we're basically saying we're going to do everything in our power to make it safely to death.

Quotes...

Are others' opinions of us more important to us than our opinions of ourselves? Do we determine who we are by looking outside or inside?

We would never accept being forced to relinquish our personal power, and yet that's exactly what many of us voluntarily do.

As workers in this evolving world of work, how often do we ruin a perfectly good present moment over some organizational change that's rumored to be occurring in six months — maybe.

Are we playing with life or working at it?

Quotes...

Certain events in our lives are labeled negative only because we have chosen to label them negative. It's not what they "are," and it's not what they have to be.

It's useless at best and frustrating at worst to set a goal whose outcome depends on somebody else.

If we're not responsible, we can't change. If we cannot change, we are not in control. If we are not in control, we're victims. If we're victims, we're unfulfilled, unproductive and unhappy.

Look for humor in your workplace because there's an awful lot of funny stuff going on.

Quotes...

Better to have failed and lost than never to have failed at all.

★

Who we are is what we think, not what we do.

★

What we give with our work is every bit as important as what we get.

When our world changes fundamentally and radically, we must change fundamentally and radically.

If being honest hurts a relationship, maybe the relationship is not as strong as it needs to be.

Quotes...

If we sit back and hold someone or something else responsible for our success, we'll be getting off the train a couple stops short of our station.

Responsibility is holding ourselves answerable for what we make of our lives.

Are we spending our time because it is there to spend , or are we spending it to accomplish our purpose?

Diversity doesn't mean we must have an office that looks like the United Nations cafeteria, but we must have diverse ideas. Diverse ideas tend to come from people with diverse backgrounds.

Quotes...

None of the changes we've gone through
or will be going through
care what we think of them.

Before you throw water over the embers of a relationship, be sure you don't need the warmth.

The term self-motivation is a redundancy — there is no other way.

Quotes...

If we're not responsible for the event, we're therefore not responsible for the result that event created. We're the perfect victims.

We never really know how much we believe in something until there is some risk involved in that belief.

No matter how important we are, sometimes we just gotta do something goofy.

Imagine the strength of the relationships and the power, energy and passion that would run loose in an organization whose core value is, "Always communicate the truth."

Quotes...

If we want to <u>be</u> something else, we need to <u>do</u> something else.

★

Maintain visibility, marketability and mobility.

★

Work should not be a four-letter word.

If there is a difference between what is said and what is done, what is done wins every time.

I believe the objective of the worker cannot be to make money, and the objective of a business must be to make money. If that belief is true, how can a non-monetarily oriented worker ever work in harmony with a monetarily oriented organization?

Quotes...

I'm about to give you the secret missing ingredient to attainment of all of your life's dreams and desires. Here it is, ready? — luck

Are we finding ourselves able to function quite well in a world that's ceased to exist?

Choose not to give your body a double message. When confused, it tends to attack.

Events have no feelings attached to them; that's our job. So if we don't like now what we did like then and continue to do what we don't like now and did like then, we've got work to do.

Quotes...

The challenge comes in our being truthful with ourselves about the present. Is our present pleasant, or is it a not-so-pleasant present?

It doesn't matter how excited, passionate and committed we are. If we can't make a living at that which we're attempting to make a living, we can't keep doing it.

Knowing where you want to go is useless unless you know where you are.

We could never hide our emotions if we had a dog's tail.

Quotes...

Fear of the unknown doesn't make sense. Now fear of the present is another story.

Never do unto others until you're sure they want it done unto them.

It's important to remember: everything we do has a price. What price are you paying for your company benefits?

The answer to how we should operate in the future may well lie with someone not of our generation or race, who does not speak our language or use the same washroom we use.

Quotes...

If we put ourselves in a position of being dependent on an organization for our security and we have no control over that organization, we therefore have no control over our security — a stressful position in which to be.

Don't look at current work and determine where you'll fit in the future — look at work the way you want work to be and create your fit.

Whatever you did yesterday
they can never take away from you.
What did you do yesterday?

Books and Programs by Tom Payne

To obtain additional information on Tom Payne and his interactive programs, or to order copies (quantity discounts available) of *Quotes for a Changing Workplace; From the Inside Out: How to Create & Survive a Culture of Change; A Company of One: The Power of Independence in the Workplace;* and/or *FutureWork: Five Rules for a New Game*, contact:

LODESTAR Ltd. Co. ★
17 Anne Court Tijeras, NM 87059-7816
800-447-9254 505-286-3729 FAX 505-286-3728
E-mail: lodestar@rt66.com
Browse: http://www.rt66.com/~lodestar/